GRAPHIC DINOSAUR

D0824645

TRICERATOPS

THE THREE HORNED DINOSAUR

ILLUSTRATED BY TERRY RILEY AND GEOFF BALL

PowerKiDS
press.

New York

EL DORADO COUNTY LIBRARY
345 FAIR LANE
PLACERVILLE, CA 95667

Published in 2008 by The Rosen Publishing Group, Inc.
29 East 21st Street, New York, NY 10010

Copyright © 2008 David West Books

All rights reserved. No part of this book may be reproduced in any form without permission in writing from the publisher, except by a reviewer.

Designed and produced by
David West Books

Designed and written by Rob Shone
Editor: Gail Bushnell
Consultant: Steve Parker, Senior Scientific Fellow, Zoological Society of London
Photographic credits: 5t, Adam Hart Davis; 5m, Witte Museum; 30, Witte Museum.

Library of Congress Cataloging-in-Publication Data

Shone, Rob.
Triceratops : the three horned dinosaur / Rob Shone.
p. cm. — (Graphic dinosaurs)
Includes index.
ISBN-13: 978-1-4042-3896-1 (library binding) ISBN-10: 1-4042-3896-4 (library binding)
ISBN-13: 978-1-4042-9626-8 (pbk.) ISBN-10: 1-4042-9626-3 (pbk.)
ISBN-13: 978-1-4042-9668-8 (6 pack) ISBN-10: 1-4042-9668-9 (6 pack)
1. Triceratops—Juvenile literature. 2. Dinosaurs—Juvenile literature. I. Title.
QE862.O65W43 2008
567.915'8—dc22
2007009374

Manufactured in China

CONTENTS

WHAT IS A TRICERATOPS?

TRICERATOPS MEANS "THREE HORNED FACE"

← Triceratops probably lived in herds.

← Triceratops's legs had to be strong to carry its huge weight.

← The frill covering its neck was made of solid bone.

← It had good eyesight, hearing, and sense of smell to help keep it out of danger.

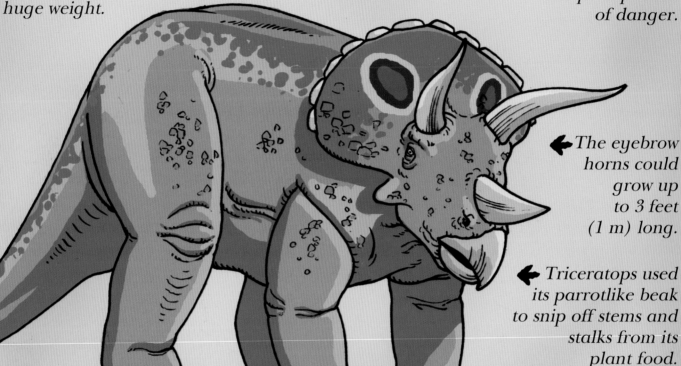

← The eyebrow horns could grow up to 3 feet (1 m) long.

← Triceratops used its parrotlike beak to snip off stems and stalks from its plant food.

← The elbows and knees stuck out sideways slightly, making it difficult to run fast.

← The teeth at the back of the mouth chopped the tough food up into small, easily swallowed pieces.

TRICERATOPS WAS A DINOSAUR THAT LIVED AROUND 70 TO 65 MILLION YEARS AGO, DURING THE **CRETACEOUS PERIOD**. **FOSSILS** OF ITS SKELETON HAVE BEEN FOUND IN NORTH AMERICA.

Adult Triceratops measured up to 30 feet (8 m) long, 10 feet (3 m) high, and weighed 10 tons (9,070 kg).

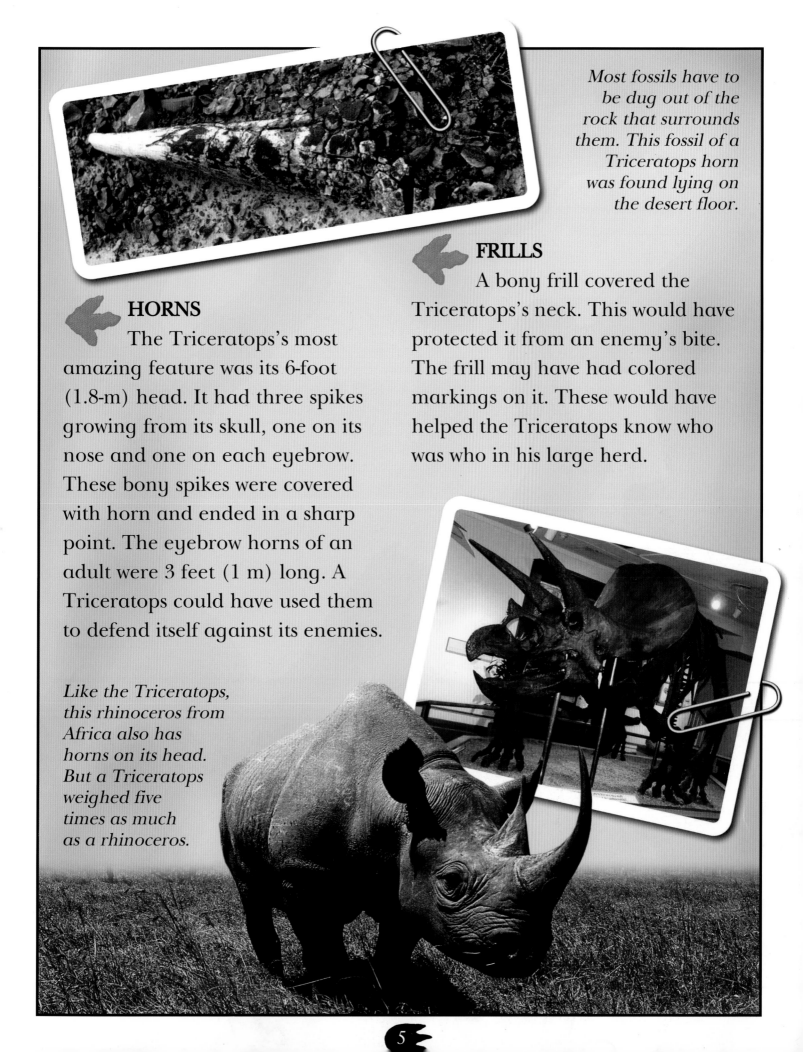

Most fossils have to be dug out of the rock that surrounds them. This fossil of a Triceratops horn was found lying on the desert floor.

FRILLS

A bony frill covered the Triceratops's neck. This would have protected it from an enemy's bite. The frill may have had colored markings on it. These would have helped the Triceratops know who was who in his large herd.

HORNS

The Triceratops's most amazing feature was its 6-foot (1.8-m) head. It had three spikes growing from its skull, one on its nose and one on each eyebrow. These bony spikes were covered with horn and ended in a sharp point. The eyebrow horns of an adult were 3 feet (1 m) long. A Triceratops could have used them to defend itself against its enemies.

Like the Triceratops, this rhinoceros from Africa also has horns on its head. But a Triceratops weighed five times as much as a rhinoceros.

PART ONE... THE RAID

THE LARGE LIZARD WAITS FOR ITS CHANCE. THE TRICERATOPS EGGS WOULD MAKE A GOOD MEAL, BUT THE PARENTS ARE GUARDING THE NEST.

THE TRICERATOPS DO NOT KNOW THAT THEY ARE BEING SPIED ON.

MOVING VERY SLOWLY, THE LIZARD CREEPS TOWARD AN UNGUARDED NEST.

SZZAAAHHHH!

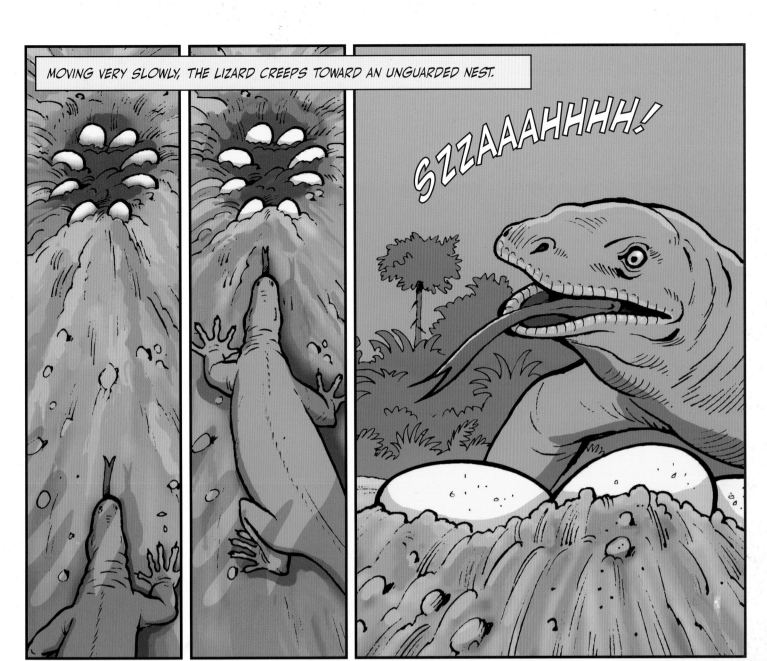

IT STEALS AN EGG, BUT BEFORE IT CAN EAT...

THE MOTHER TRICERATOPS TURNS BACK TO HER NEST JUST IN TIME.

BROOAAARR!!!

THE MOTHER'S ROAR ALERTS THE REST OF THE HERD.

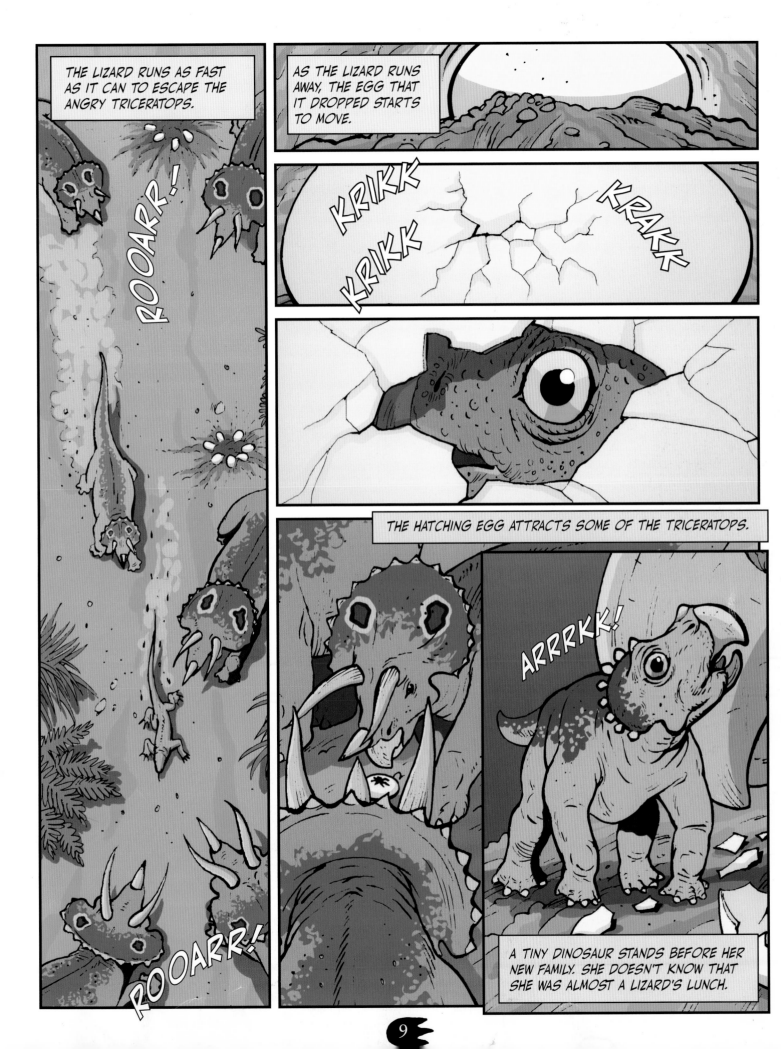

THE LIZARD RUNS AS FAST AS IT CAN TO ESCAPE THE ANGRY TRICERATOPS.

ROOARR!

ROOARR!

AS THE LIZARD RUNS AWAY, THE EGG THAT IT DROPPED STARTS TO MOVE.

KRIKK

KRIKK

KRAKK

THE HATCHING EGG ATTRACTS SOME OF THE TRICERATOPS.

ARRRKK!

A TINY DINOSAUR STANDS BEFORE HER NEW FAMILY. SHE DOESN'T KNOW THAT SHE WAS ALMOST A LIZARD'S LUNCH.

PART TWO

LOST

A YEAR HAS PASSED. THE SMALL TRICERATOPS SPENDS HER DAYS WITH THE REST OF THE HERD, *GRAZING* ON FERNS AND SHRUBS.

THERE IS PLENTY OF FOOD IN THE HERD'S OPEN WOODLAND HOME. SHE HAS GROWN QUICKLY AND IS NOW NEARLY 3 FEET (1 M) LONG. THE HERD IS MOVING FROM HIGHER GROUND TO THE RIVER PLAIN BELOW.

THE TRICERATOPS LIVE ALONGSIDE OTHER DINOSAURS. GIANT PLANT-EATERS, LIKE THE LONG-NECKED ALAMOSAURUS AND THE CREST-HEADED PARASAUROLOPHUS, WANDER THROUGH THE LANDSCAPE.

SMALLER DINOSAURS LIVE NEARBY TOO, LIKE THE BONY-HEADED STEGOCERAS AND THE BEAKED ORNITHOMIMUS. THEY DO NOT BOTHER THE LARGE TRICERATOPS.

BUT NOT ALL DINOSAURS ARE HARMLESS. TWO MEAT-EATING DROMAEOSAURUS ARE WATCHING THE LITTLE DINOSAUR. THEY ARE WAITING FOR A CHANCE TO ATTACK.

TWO ANKYLOSAURS APPROACH THE FEEDING TRICERATOPS.

BROOARRKK!

THE ANKYLOSAURS ARE NOT MEAT-EATERS, BUT THEIR HEAVY, SWINGING TAILS COULD HURT A YOUNG TRICERATOPS. ONE OF THE ADULT TRICERATOPS SHAKES ITS HUGE HEAD AND ROARS AT THE ANKYLOSAURS UNTIL THEY SLOWLY MOVE OFF.

THE HERD DOESN'T NOTICE THAT THE SMALL DINOSAUR HAS STRAYED.

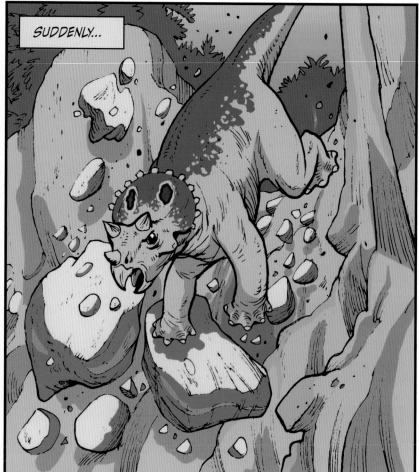

SUDDENLY...

SHHLUMPH!

THE TRICERATOPS FINDS HERSELF AT THE BOTTOM OF A STEEP-SIDED *RAVINE.* SHE CALLS OUT TO THE HERD, BUT THERE IS NO REPLY.

WAAARRKK!

SHE IS SURROUNDED BY A DARK, DENSE WOOD. IT IS A STRANGE NEW WORLD TO HER. LOUD ANIMAL CALLS ECHO AMONG THE TREES...

KEE! KEE! KEE!

...WHILE INSECTS AND LIZARDS SLITHER OVER THE JUNGLE FLOOR.

CRACKLE! SNAP!

SHE HEARS RUSTLING. SOMETHING IS COMING.

SHE HIDES, NOT DARING TO MOVE.

THE SOUND GETS CLOSER...

...AND CLOSER.

A DIDELPHODON APPEARS. IT ISN'T A DINOSAUR BUT AN ANCIENT MAMMAL.

WAARRRKKARRK!!

SKREEK!!

BOTH ANIMALS ARE SURPRISED.

THE DINOSAUR AND THE MAMMAL CHARGE THROUGH THE UNDERGROWTH.

THE TRICERATOPS RUNS UNTIL SHE COMES TO A MARSHY POOL.

SHE FEELS HUNGRY AND BEGINS TO EAT.

THE POOL IS NOT AS QUIET AS IT LOOKS THOUGH.

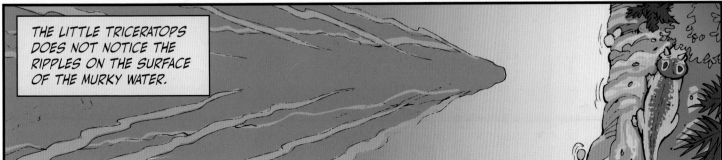

THE LITTLE TRICERATOPS DOES NOT NOTICE THE RIPPLES ON THE SURFACE OF THE MURKY WATER.

IT SNAPS A SECOND TIME, BUT THE TRICERATOPS DODGES AWAY...

...AND RUNS, CRASHING THROUGH THE THICK JUNGLE.

WAAARRK!

THEN, SUDDENLY, THE LITTLE DINOSAUR BURSTS OUT OF THE DARK WOODS.

WAAAARRK!

THE REST OF THE HERD HAS REACHED THE PLAIN AND IS NOT FAR AWAY. SHE SEES THEM AND WITH A CRY RUSHES TO JOIN THEM. FROM NOW ON, SHE WILL STAY CLOSE TO THE ADULTS TO KEEP SAFE.

PART THREE... THE LANDSLIDE

IT IS THE WET SEASON, AND THE LITTLE DINOSAUR IS FIVE YEARS OLD.

SHE IS NOW OVER 7 FEET (2 M) LONG. THE TRICERATOPS DO NOT MIND BEING WET, BUT THE COOLING RAIN MAKES THEM FEEL *SLUGGISH.*

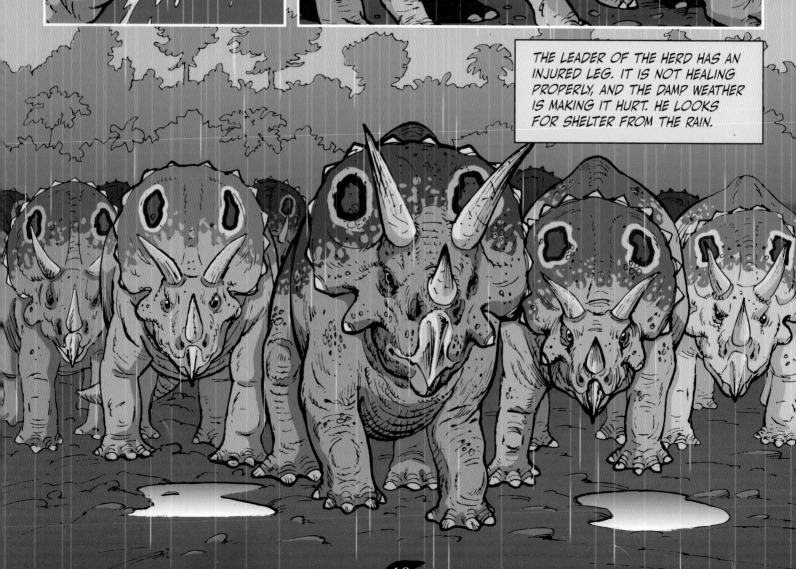

THE LEADER OF THE HERD HAS AN INJURED LEG. IT IS NOT HEALING PROPERLY, AND THE DAMP WEATHER IS MAKING IT HURT. HE LOOKS FOR SHELTER FROM THE RAIN.

HE LEADS THE HERD TO THE FOOT OF A CLIFF FACE. THE OVERHANGING ROCKS WILL GIVE THEM SOME PROTECTION FROM THE RAIN.

TWO THESCELOSAURS ARE ALREADY THERE. THEY MOVE WHEN THEY SEE THE HERD COMING TOWARD THEM.

IT RAINS EVEN HARDER. AT THE TOP OF THE CLIFF, SMALL STONES AND SOIL BECOME LOOSE IN THE RUSH OF WATER.

SOON, EVEN LARGER ROCKS START TO FALL DOWN THE CLIFF FACE.

INSTEAD OF PROVIDING SHELTER FOR THE HERD, THE BIG ROCKS GIVE WAY AND MAY CRUSH IT.

THE HERD IS IN DANGER...

...AND RUNS.

BUT THE HURT OLD LEADER CANNOT MOVE QUICKLY ENOUGH.

KERRUMMPPP!

HE IS BURIED UNDER MANY TONS OF ROCK AND MUD.

SEVERAL DAYS LATER THE RAIN STOPS. THE HERD ENJOYS THE WARMER WEATHER. THE SMALLEST TRICERATOPS START TO PLAY-FIGHT WITH EACH OTHER.

BOUFF!

THE YOUNG TRICERATOPS WATCHES THE ADULTS. THEY ARE NOT FEEDING AND STAND TOGETHER IN A GROUP.

ARRKK!

THEY ARE CHOOSING A NEW LEADER. IT WILL BE THE STRONGEST MALE IN THE HERD. THE MALES ROAR AND SHAKE THEIR FRILLED HEADS AT EACH OTHER TO SHOW OFF THEIR SIZE AND STRENGTH.

ROAARRR!

ONE BY ONE THE MALES BACK DOWN UNTIL THERE ARE JUST TWO TRICERATOPS LEFT—THE LARGEST. THE TWO GIANT ANIMALS ARE EVENLY MATCHED AND NEITHER WILL GIVE IN.

THEY FIGHT TO SEE WHO WILL BECOME LEADER.

DUHTHUNKK!

WITH THEIR HORNS LOCKED, THEY PUSH AND SHOVE...

SNORT!!

...TRYING TO PROVE WHICH IS THE STRONGER.

FINALLY, ONE TRICERATOPS BREAKS AWAY, BEATEN.

BRROOAAARR!!

THE WINNER BELLOWS TO LET THE HERD KNOW IT HAS A NEW LEADER.

PART FOUR... HUNTED

THE NEW LEADER IS TAKING THE HERD TO FIND A BETTER FEEDING GROUND. A DASPLETOSAURUS HAS BEEN FOLLOWING THEM FOR SOME TIME. THE CARNIVORE IS MAKING THEM NERVOUS.

A SINGLE DASPLETOSAURUS IS NOT A DANGER TO THE HERD OR TO AN ADULT TRICERATOPS. BUT IT COULD KILL A STRAY *JUVENILE* IF IT GOT CLOSE ENOUGH.

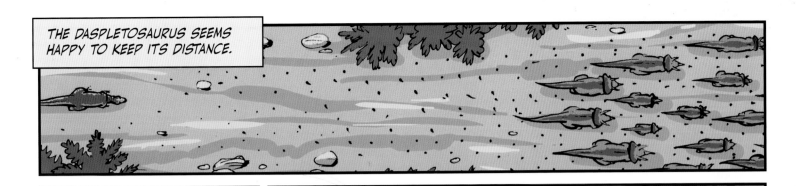

THE DASPLETOSAURUS SEEMS HAPPY TO KEEP ITS DISTANCE.

BUT THE HERD IS NOT TAKING ANY CHANCES. ADULT MALES MOVE TO THE REAR TO KEEP A CLOSE WATCH ON THE MEAT-EATER.

MWAAAURR.!

THE YOUNG TRICERATOPS IS IN THE MIDDLE OF THE HERD. SHE IS EIGHT YEARS OLD AND NEARLY 13 FEET (4 M) LONG, BUT SHE IS STILL A JUVENILE.

SUDDENLY, FROM THEIR HIDING PLACE...

HZARRKH!

...THREE SMALL DASPLETOSAURUS RUSH AT THE HERD LEADERS. THE TRICERATOPS HAVE BEEN LED INTO A TRAP. THEY STAND IN LINE, DISPLAYING A WALL OF HORNS.

THE YOUNG DASPLETOSAURUS ARE NO MATCH FOR ADULT TRICERATOPS...

...BUT THEIR PLAN IS NOT OVER.

ANOTHER DASPLETOSAURUS, THE LARGEST, BURSTS FROM THE TREES.

IT HAS CHOSEN ITS VICTIM—AN UNGUARDED JUVENILE. ALL IT WILL TAKE TO KILL IT IS ONE GOOD BITE.

GRRAHH!

THE LARGE DASPLETOSAURUS CLOSES IN ON ITS PREY.

MEANWHILE, THE SMALLEST DASPLETOSAURUS...

...HAS SLIPPED THROUGH THE WALL OF WAVING HORNS.

IT SEES THE LITTLE TRICERATOPS...

GNARRSK!

...AND CHASES AFTER HER.

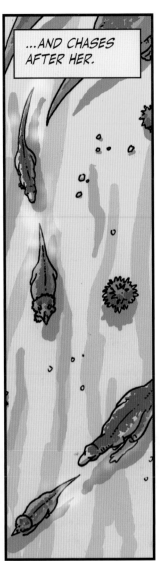

THE SCARED TRICERATOPS RUNS AS FAST AS SHE CAN...

ARRKKK!

...BUT FORGETS TO LOOK WHERE SHE IS GOING.

UNTIL...

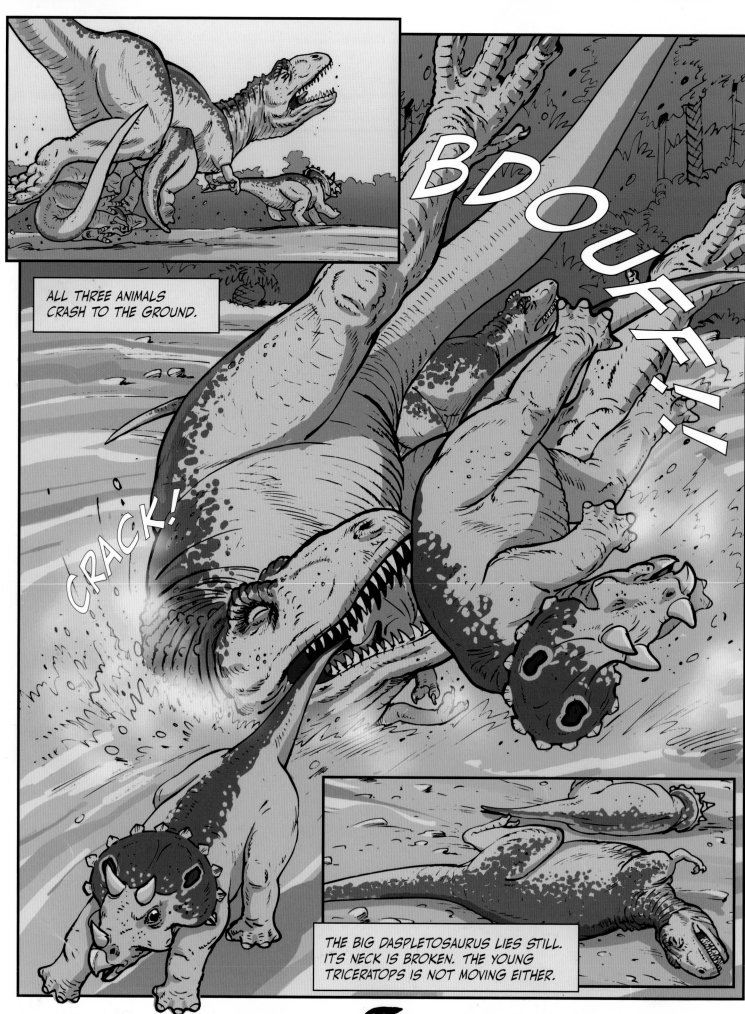

ALL THREE ANIMALS CRASH TO THE GROUND.

BDOUFF!!

CRACK!

THE BIG DASPLETOSAURUS LIES STILL. ITS NECK IS BROKEN. THE YOUNG TRICERATOPS IS NOT MOVING EITHER.

THE PACK OF DASPLETOSAURUS WALKS AWAY.

THE YOUNG TRICERATOPS DOES NOT MOVE AT ALL. THE HERD WAITS UNTIL THE DASPLETOSAURUS HAVE GONE. THEN THEY LEAVE.

LATER.

BLINK

BLINK

THE YOUNG TRICERATOPS IS NOT DEAD, JUST KNOCKED OUT. SHE WAKES UP AND STRUGGLES TO HER FEET.

SHE HAS SURVIVIED ANOTHER AMAZING ADVENTURE AND KNOWS WHAT SHE MUST DO. SHE CANNOT SEE THE HERD, BUT SHE CAN SMELL IT. THE TOUGH YOUNG DINOSAUR HURRIES TO REJOIN HER HERD, WHERE SHE WILL BE SAFE ONCE MORE.

WAARRKK!

FOSSIL EVIDENCE

SCIENTISTS LEARN WHAT DINOSAURS MAY HAVE LOOKED LIKE BY STUDYING THEIR FOSSIL REMAINS. FOSSILS ARE FORMED WHEN THE HARD PARTS OF AN ANIMAL OR PLANT BECOME BURIED AND TURN TO ROCK OVER MILLIONS OF YEARS.

The fossilized bones of a dinosaur tell us what shape and size it was. Sometimes they can tell us how that dinosaur lived. One fossilized Triceratops skull had scratch marks on its frill. Scientists think they were caused by the eyebrow horns of another Triceratops. This tells them that Triceratops sometimes fought each other.

Scientists even look at the inside of fossil skulls. Sometimes a space is left where the brain was. The space is the same shape as the brain, so we can tell from its size how smart the animal was. This is how we know that Triceratops had good senses of smell and sight, and that they had average **intelligence** for a dinosaur.

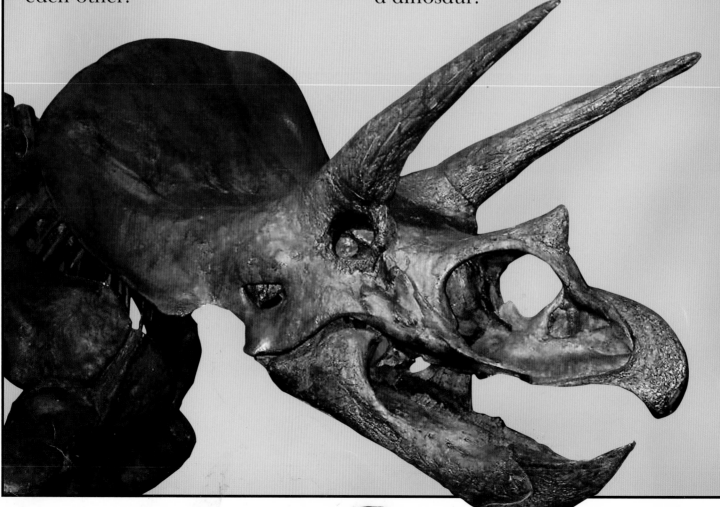

DINOSAUR GALLERY

ALL THESE ANIMALS APPEAR IN THE STORY.

Didelphodon
"Two womb teeth"
Length: 3 ft (1 m)
A small meat-eating mammal.

Dromaeosaurus
"Running lizard"
Length: 6 ft (1.8 m)
A small meat-eating dinosaur with a large curved claw on the big toe of each foot.

Stegoceras
"Horned roof"
Length: 7 ft (2 m)
A small plant-eating dinosaur with a very thick, bony skull.

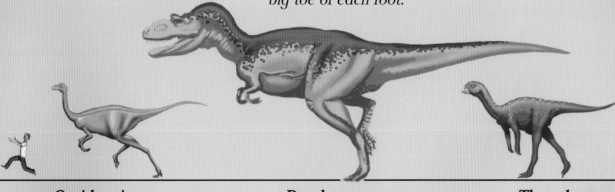

Ornithomimus
"Bird mimic"
Length: 15 ft (4.6 m)
A fast-running, meat-eating dinosaur with a bony, toothless beak.

Daspletosaurus
"Horrible lizard"
Length: 28 ft (8.5 m)
A large meat-eating dinosaur with two tiny arms and weighing 3 tons (2,730 kg).

Thescelosaurus
"Marvelous lizard"
Length: 13 ft (4 m)
A fast-running, plant-eating dinosaur with a parrotlike beak.

Parasaurolophus
"Near crested lizard"
Length: 33 ft (10 m)
A plant-eating dinosaur with a long tube-shaped head crest.

Alamosaurus
"Alamo lizard"
Length: 68 ft (21 m)
A giant plant-eating dinosaur weighing 30 tons (27,200 kg).

Ankylosaurus
"Fused lizard"
Length: 33 ft (10 m)
An armored dinosaur with a bony club on the end of its tail.

GLOSSARY

carnivore (KAHR-nuh-vor) A meat-eating animal.

Cretaceous period (krih-TAY-shus PIR-ee-ud) The time between 146 million and 65 million years ago.

fossils (FAH-sulz) The remains of living things that have turned to rock.

grazing (GRAYZ-ing) Feeding on low-growing plants.

intelligence (in-TEH-luh-jents) How smart an animal is.

juvenile (JOO-veh-ny-uhl) A young animal that is not fully grown.

prey (PRAY) Animals that are hunted for food by another animal.

ravine (ruh-VEEN) A deep and narrow valley with steep sides.

sluggish (SLUH-gish) Moving and thinking slowly.

INDEX

Web Sites

Due to the changing nature of Internet links, the Rosen Publishing Group, Inc., has developed an online list of Web sites related to the subject of this book. This site is updated regularly. Please use this link to access the list:

www.powerkidslinks.com/gdino/tricer/

JUN 2 6 2009